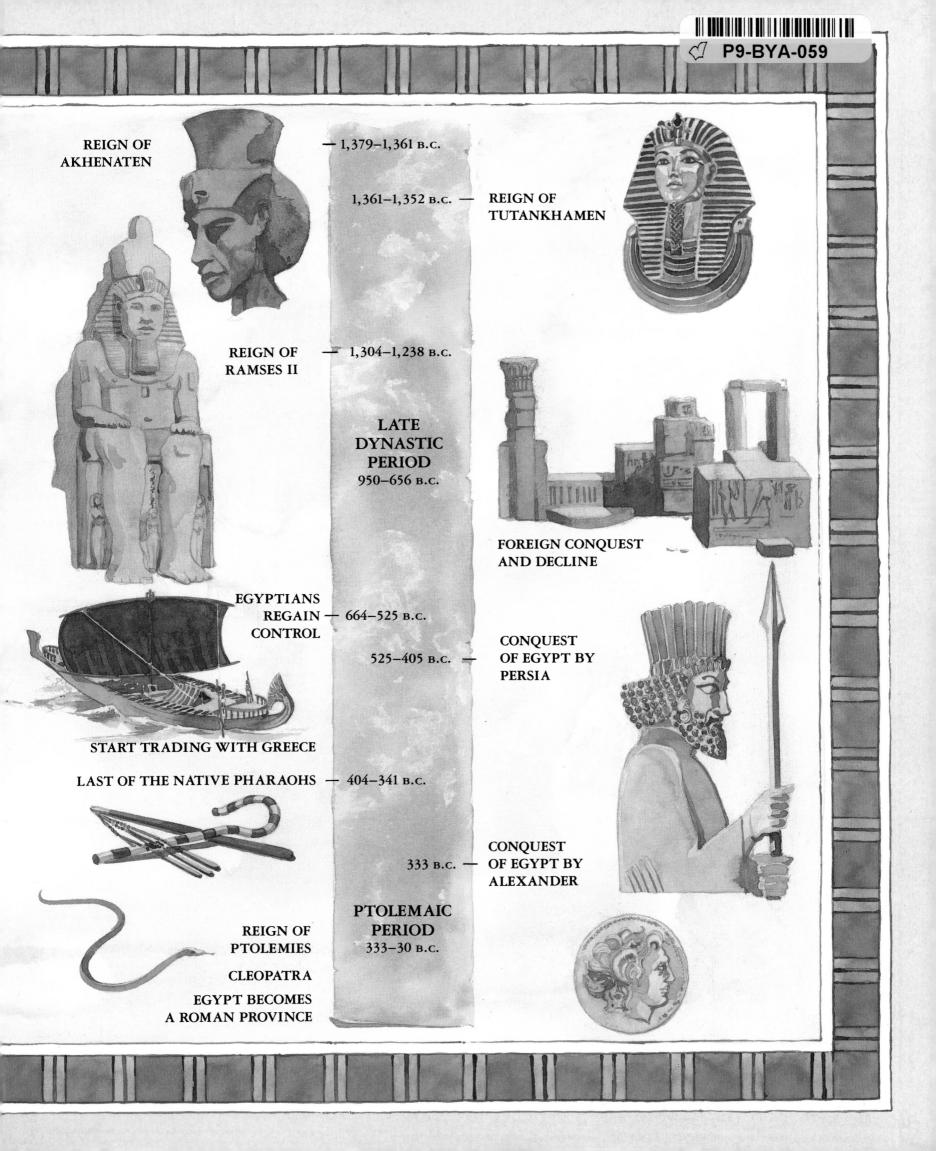

REIGN OF
AKHENATEN

— 1,379–1,361 B.C.

1,361–1,352 B.C. —

REIGN OF
TUTANKHAMEN

REIGN OF
RAMSES II

— 1,304–1,238 B.C.

LATE
DYNASTIC
PERIOD
950–656 B.C.

FOREIGN CONQUEST
AND DECLINE

EGYPTIANS
REGAIN
CONTROL

— 664–525 B.C.

525–405 B.C. —

CONQUEST
OF EGYPT BY
PERSIA

START TRADING WITH GREECE

LAST OF THE NATIVE PHARAOHS — 404–341 B.C.

CONQUEST
OF EGYPT BY
ALEXANDER

333 B.C. —

PTOLEMAIC
PERIOD
333–30 B.C.

REIGN OF
PTOLEMIES

CLEOPATRA

EGYPT BECOMES
A ROMAN PROVINCE

By Daniel Cohen
Illustrated by Gary A. Lippincott

ANCIENT EGYPT

Doubleday

New York   London   Toronto   Sydney   Auckland

Other books you will enjoy:

Sharks by Gilda Berger
Dinosaurs by Daniel Cohen
Whales by Gilda Berger
Prehistoric Animals
　by Daniel Cohen
Stars and Planets
　by Christopher Lampton
The Human Body
　by Gilda Berger

**For Nicholas Milton Fuller
D. C.**

The editor wishes to thank Dr. James Romano, Egyptologist, The Brooklyn Museum, for his careful review of the manuscript and artwork.

Published by Doubleday,
a division of
Bantam Doubleday Dell Publishing Group, Inc., 666 Fifth Avenue, New York, New York 10103

Doubleday
and the portrayal of an anchor with a dolphin are trademarks of Doubleday, a division of Bantam Doubleday Dell Publishing Group, Inc.
Library of Congress Cataloging-in-Publication Data
Cohen, Daniel.
　　Ancient Egypt / by Daniel Cohen; illustrated by Gary A. Lippincott.—1st ed.
　　　　p.　cm.
　　Includes index.
　　Summary: Explores the daily life, customs, and achievements of the ancient Egyptians.
　　ISBN 0-385-24586-6
　　ISBN 0-385-24587-4 (lib. bdg.)
　　1. Egypt—Civilization—To 332 B.C.—Juvenile literature. [1. Egypt—Civilization—To 332 B.C.] I. Lippincott, Gary A., ill. II. Title.
DT61.C55　1990
932—dc19　88-12146　CIP　AC

"I See Wonderful Things…"

A small hole had been made in the sealed door. As the crowd waited anxiously, Howard Carter thrust a candle through the opening and peered in. The candle flickered in the hot air and at first he could see nothing. Then his eyes became accustomed to the darkness. He saw "strange animals, statues, and gold—everywhere the glint of gold." For a moment he was too astonished to speak.

Finally Lord Carnarvon, who was standing by his side, asked, "Can you see anything?"

"Yes," he replied, ". . . wonderful things."

That is how archaeologist Howard Carter described the opening of the tomb of King Tutankhamen on November 26, 1922. The discovery of the tomb of this ancient Egyptian king ranks as the greatest archaeological discovery of modern times. The treasures in the tomb astonished everyone. Just a few years ago, when a small portion of these treasures were sent on a world tour, people lined up for hours just to catch a glimpse of objects from "King Tut's" tomb.

Yet King Tutankhamen was a very minor king or pharaoh. The golden glory of his tomb is only a pale reflection of the true glory of that most long-lived and amazing of all ancient civilizations—Egypt.

The Nile

The land of Egypt was created by the Nile River. The river begins in Central Africa where there is abundant rain. It flows northward through a thousand miles of parched desert to the Mediterranean Sea. Just before it reaches the Mediterranean the river spreads out into many branches, forming what is called the delta. Once a year the mountains at the source of the Nile are swept by torrential rainstorms. The rains swell the river and in Egypt it overflows its banks in an annual flood.

For most people a flood is a disaster. For the people of Egypt it has been a blessing. The floodwaters of the Nile bring with them fertile mud. When the waters recede the people can plant their crops in the rich soil, which is renewed every year. Perpetual sunshine does the rest. In ancient times the six hundred miles bordering the Nile in Egypt was the most productive farmland in the world. It's no wonder that thousands of years ago people chose to settle along the Nile.

But the Nile could not always be relied upon. Some years the flood would be low. In other years the flood would be so great that it would sweep away whole villages. The water had to be controlled, so canals, dikes, and reservoirs were built. Records of the time and extent of the flooding had to be kept to see if a pattern was being established. Desert nomads who envied the prosperous Nile farmers had to be fought off. All of this took organization. The more organized the people of the Nile became, the more they prospered.

CANAAN

RED
SEA

King of
the Two Lands

Before the recorded history of
Egypt began, the people of the
Nile were divided into forty or
so small independent districts.
Gradually these districts were united
into two major states, Upper and
Lower Egypt. Upper Egypt was the
long, fertile strip that borders the Nile.
Lower Egypt was the delta region. The
names can be confusing because when
you look at a map the delta or Lower
Egypt is at the top, while Upper Egypt
is below it.

Around 5,200 years ago a king of
Upper Egypt, called Narmer,
conquered Lower Egypt and unified the
two lands. Narmer was a fierce warrior
who lived in a savage age. Two pictures
of him still exist. One shows him
smashing the skull of a wounded
opponent with a heavy club. In the
other he is parading before piles of the
headless corpses of his enemies.

Narmer set a pattern of ruling that
was to last for three thousand years.
The king was not only absolute ruler,
he was a living god. Egypt continued to
be ruled by god-kings from the time of
Narmer until the land was taken over
by the Roman Empire in 30 B.C. The
Kingdom of Ancient Egypt lasted
longer than any other civilization the
world has ever known.

Of course there were changes in
Egypt over thirty centuries. But change
came very slowly. One of the most
remarkable changes came in the way
the early kings were buried.

Imhotep—
The First Genius

The early god-kings of Egypt and many of their nobles were buried under or inside sloping rectangular brick structures known as mastabas. An exceptionally powerful king named Zoser decided that his tomb should be something far grander. The project was put in the hands of Zoser's chief counselor, Imhotep.

Imhotep was a remarkable man. For centuries he was renowned as an architect, a physician, a priest, a magician, a writer and a maker of wise sayings. Egyptians would often begin some piece of advice with the words, "Imhotep says . . ." Twenty-five hundred years after his death, Imhotep was worshiped by the Egyptians and Greeks as a god.

We don't really know anything about Imhotep's accomplishments in most of these fields. But we do know about his work as an architect. He started by designing a very large stone mastaba for Zoser. Then there was a change of plans. Three smaller mastabas were built on top of the first. Then plans changed again. The whole structure was enlarged and two successively smaller mastabas were built on top of the first four. The result, which still stands today, was a six-tiered stepped pyramid that towered some 200 feet above the desert at Sakkara. Beneath the solid pyramid was a maze of underground tunnels and chambers, one of which was the king's burial chamber. The Step Pyramid was surrounded by a walled enclosure the length of six football fields, containing temples and courtyards where ceremonies in honor of the dead king could be performed.

Nothing remotely like the Step Pyramid had ever been built anywhere. Small wonder that later ages regarded Imhotep as a god.

The Bent Pyramid after many years of wear

The Pyramid Age

Imhotep's creation inspired an era of pyramid building. Up and down the Nile the kings of Egypt had pyramids constructed for their tombs. Perhaps because these projects did not have the driving force of a genius like Imhotep behind them, many were failures. They were either left unfinished or were so poorly constructed that they have fallen apart.

At a spot called Meidum are the remains of what looks like another stepped pyramid. It is surrounded by a mass of broken stone. Scientists believe that the builders tried to construct a smooth-sided true pyramid. They started with a stepped pyramid and filled in the steps with blocks of stone. But the structure wasn't stable. At some point, the outside stones slipped off in a catastrophic accident. All that is left is the original steps.

At a place called Dashur is an example of a pyramid that was not built as originally planned. This structure is called the Bent Pyramid. The original plan called for the pyramid to rise at a fairly steep angle. About one third of the way up the angle was changed to a much shallower one. No one knows why. Perhaps the builders were afraid that a pyramid built on such a steep angle was unstable.

The Bent Pyramid was probably built for King Snefru who died in 2592 B.C. He was a king of enormous power, and apparently a popular ruler as well. For centuries when Egyptians wanted to refer to "the good old days" they would say, "In the days of King Snefru . . ."

Snefru had a second pyramid built for himself. This pyramid was not bent and it did not collapse. By trial and error Egyptian engineers mastered the art of pyramid building.

The stage was now set for the construction of the most famous Egyptian monument, probably the most famous monument in the history of the world—the Great Pyramid at Giza, just outside the modern city of Cairo.

The Great Pyramid

The Great Pyramid was built by King Khufu. Khufu was Snefru's successor. He ruled Egypt for about twenty-five years. While legend holds that Snefru was a good and wise king, Khufu was known as a tyrant. He wanted a tomb that would be grander than any that had ever been built before.

Khufu's pyramid is a man-made mountain. It stands nearly 500 feet high and each side is over 750 feet long at ground level. The Great Pyramid is the largest tomb ever built and the largest structure of any kind to be built before modern times.

Even today, after nearly five thousand years, the Great Pyramid is awesome. But now much of its beauty is gone. Originally the pyramid was covered by a layer of polished white limestone. The surface was smooth and gleaming from top to bottom. The pyramid was surrounded by a virtual city of tombs and temples. Over the centuries the limestone was stripped away and used to build the city of Cairo. The smaller tombs and temples have fallen into ruin.

At Giza there are two other pyramids built by Khufu's successors. The pyramid of King Chephren is slightly smaller, though it looks larger at a distance because it is built on higher ground. The third pyramid, that of Menkaure, is much smaller. That may indicate that the wealth and power of the pharaohs were declining, or simply that the Egyptians decided to use their wealth in other ways. Pyramid building was a huge and expensive task.

The Giant Sphinx

When the builders of the Great Pyramid finished cutting the stone they needed, there was still a large outcrop of rock left at Giza. The builders of the second Giza pyramid, that of Chephren, carved the rock into a huge figure of a lion with a human head. The face was that of King Chephren himself. This figure is called the sphinx, or more properly the Giant Sphinx, for there are thousands of sphinx statues in Egypt. The one at Giza is the biggest.

While the Giant Sphinx was meant to be a guardian and protector of the pyramids, many Egyptians regarded it as having the power of a god. Between the paws of the sphinx is a slab of red granite put up by a later king, Thutmose IV. It tells the story of how this king, before he came to the throne, had been out hunting. At noon he rested in the shadow of the Giant Sphinx and fell asleep. He dreamed that the sphinx spoke to him and promised him the crown of Egypt if he would clear away the sand that nearly covered its body. The prince did so and in a few years became king.

The Giant Sphinx was originally covered with plaster and painted bright colors. Over the centuries the figure has been worn down by nature and sometimes by the deliberate actions of man. A cannon shot knocked its nose off. Two large slabs of rock fell from it early in 1988. Still, this battered colossus remains one of the most striking and familiar of all Egyptian monuments.

How Were They Built?

For centuries people have looked at the pyramids and been astonished. They have wondered how the Egyptians, who had only simple tools, could have built such gigantic monuments. People have speculated about all sorts of supposedly magical "secrets of the pyramids." Some have even suggested that beings from outer space helped to build the pyramids. Scientists don't think much of that idea.

Archaeologists—scientists who study life in ancient times—do not know exactly how the pyramids were built, but they have a pretty good idea. The key was the ability to organize a large number of workmen over a long period of time.

During the annual flood the Nile would have reached nearly to the base of the Great Pyramid. Stones could have been floated down the river on rafts and dragged to the site by gangs of laborers. As the pyramid rose, a ramp was built alongside and the blocks were dragged up the ramp. An average block in the Great Pyramid weighs two and a half tons. Ten men could drag such a block along level ground. Twice that number would have been needed to pull it up a ramp.

Near the Great Pyramid, archaeologists have located the remains of housing for about four thousand workmen. These would have been the permanent staff—the engineers who planned and directed the pyramid building, and the stonecutters. At certain times of year the number of common laborers—the fellows who actually dragged the stones—may have been as high as one hundred thousand.

The laborers were not slaves. They were farmers who worked on the pyramids only during the flood season, when they could not cultivate their fields.

Did these laborers regard their backbreaking work as a heavy burden imposed on them by a hated tyrant? Or was it thought of as a sacred duty to build a monument to their king and god?

We do not know what they thought. But the workmen must have been proud of their work. Some of the work teams inscribed names like "Vigorous Gang" or "Boat Gang" on the stones they moved.

Picture Writing

Besides pyramids and sphinx statues, the Egyptians are known for having developed a form of picture writing called hieroglyphics. In the earliest times the Egyptians, like most other ancient peoples, drew pictures to communicate. A cow was represented by a picture of a cow's head. A picture of an eye stood for the word "eye." But simple pictures had limits. How, for example, could you write the king's name?

Then the Egyptians made a discovery: Use the *sounds* of words, not their *meanings.* In the Nile there is a fish called the *nar.* A chisel, to the Egyptian, was *mer.* Put the pictures together and pronounce the sounds *Nar-mer*—and you have the name Narmer, the unifier of Egypt.

Fully formed hieroglyphics were usually chiseled into the walls of temples and tombs. The Egyptians also developed simplified hieroglyphics called hieratic. This was used by scribes for ordinary writing. Most people in Egypt could not write, so there was a large group of scribes, or professional writers. Scribes wrote with brush and ink on paper made from the papyrus plant.

Hieroglyphics

The Rosetta stone

After the fall of Ancient Egypt people adopted the language of their conquerors. Hieroglyphic and hieratic Egyptian were forgotten. There were thousands of inscriptions, hundreds of thousands of papyrus rolls, but for centuries no one knew what the writing meant. In 1799 a flat stone with three inscriptions was found at the Egyptian town of Rosetta. One of the inscriptions was in Greek. Another was in Egyptian hieroglyphics and the third in a shorthand form of hieratic. All three inscriptions said the same thing. The stone dated from a time late in Egyptian history when Greek was widely used, but when the ancient forms of writing were still used as well.

A brilliant young Frenchman named Jean François Champollion was able to match the word in Greek, which he could read, to the same word in hieroglyphic and hieratic Egyptian. It was like figuring out a code. The full translation of the Ancient Egyptian language took years of hard work and the efforts of many scholars. But the Rosetta stone had provided the key and Champollion was the first to use that key.

Today the Ancient Egyptians are able to speak to us once again.

The Mummies

Very early in Egypt's history the dead were buried in shallow pits. The dry sand preserved the bodies to an astonishing degree. As Egyptian civilization developed, methods of preserving bodies became more complicated. The result was the carefully wrapped mummies which still fascinate and sometimes scare us today.

Perhaps you've see a movie where a mummy walks, dragging its wrappings behind it. That idea was made up by modern horror story writers. The ancient Egyptians didn't think mummies were supposed to walk. Most mummies have their legs and arms wrapped tightly against the body. If a mummy could be magically brought back to life, it could do no more than roll around on the ground!

Embalming royal corpses or those of high officials was a long process but not a mysterious one. The corpse was opened and all the internal organs except the heart were removed. It was then soaked in a preservative solution for about two months. After that the corpse was thoroughly dried, stuffed with straw or rags, and carefully

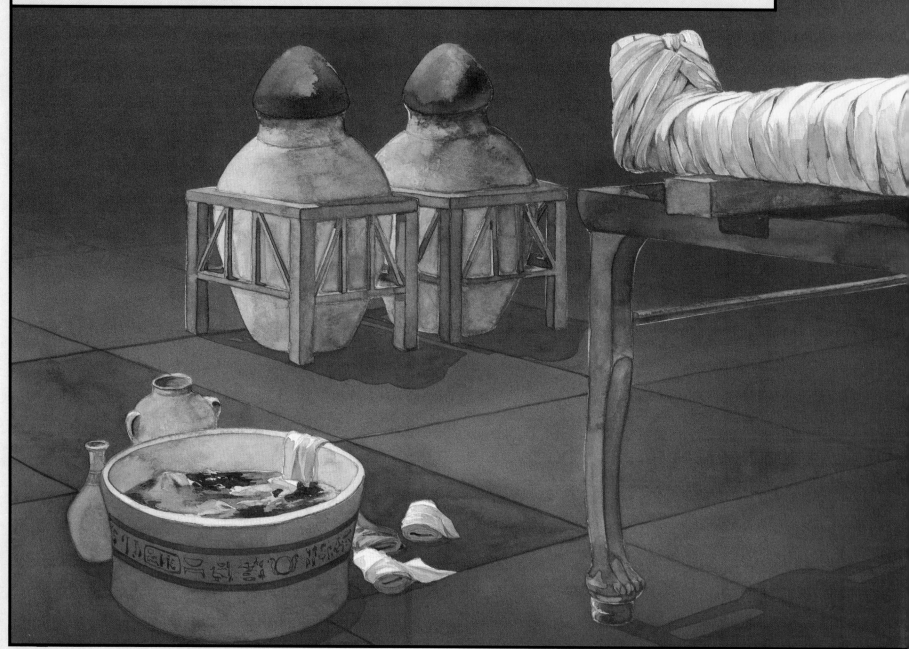

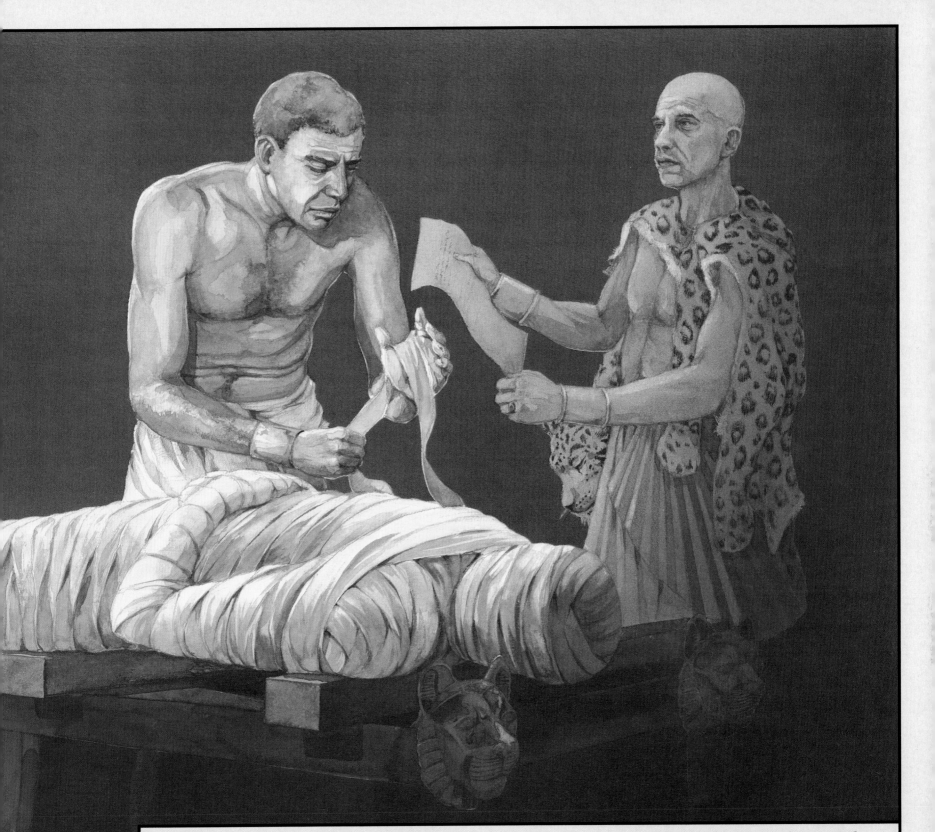

wrapped in strips of linen that had been dipped in a sticky substance called resin.

The preparation took months. Each step was accompanied by elaborate magical rituals. There were different spells to be chanted during the wrapping of each finger and toe. But the real "secret" to the preservation of Egyptian mummies was the land's hot, dry climate.

Sometimes the embalming process was less successful and even damaged the body. For example, the priests who prepared King Tutankhamen's corpse used too much resin, which hardened and stuck to the mummy. On the other hand, the mummy of King Seti I was marvelously preserved. When archaeologist Kurt Lange looked at it he commented that he knew many people still alive "who looked more decayed."

A Land of Many Gods

"There seem to be more gods than men in Egypt," an ancient Greek traveler wrote. The Egyptians worshiped a large and, to us, confusing collection of gods. Above all were the great gods like Re, the sun god. In Egypt where the sun shines every day it's easy to see why he was the chief god. There was a host of minor gods and goddesses too. Each town, each profession, each family had its own favorites.

Egyptians represented their gods in many forms—sometimes as humans, sometimes as animals, and sometimes as strange combinations of human and animal. Anubis, a god of the dead, was shown as either a jackal or a jackal-headed man. Thoth, the god of wisdom, was a man with the head of an ibis, a bird with a slender, curved beak.

Though animals were often identified with gods, they were not actually worshiped until fairly late in Egypt's history. Then travelers reacted with amazement at the huge numbers of sacred crocodiles, bulls, and birds that were lovingly tended by priests.

It was the cat that held a special place in Egyptian worship. Cats were first domesticated in Egypt, where they have always been popular. They were useful, too; cats killed the mice and rats that ate grain. A cat would be among the first rescued from a burning house. The penalty for killing a sacred cat was death. When a favorite cat died, the whole family went into mourning, and the cat was mummified. Huge cat cemeteries have been found throughout

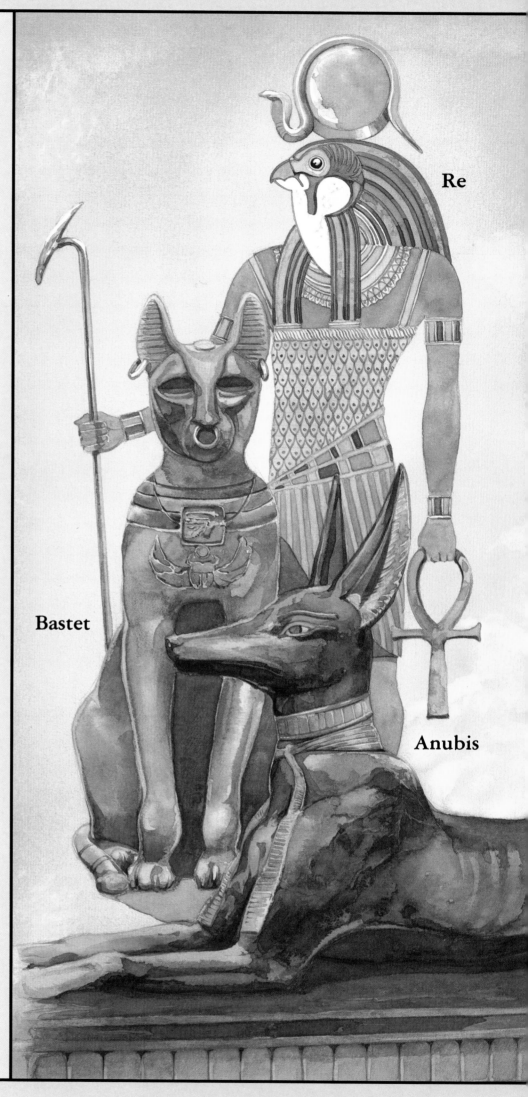

Re

Bastet

Anubis

Egypt. One at Thebes contained the mummies of hundreds of thousands of cats.

Osiris and Isis

Among the stories of the gods of Egypt the one that was repeated most often was that of Osiris and his wife Isis. Osiris was the grandson of Re and, according to the myth, one of the early kings of Egypt. Osiris was a wise and humane ruler. He persuaded the ferocious Egyptians to give up practices like cannibalism, and he taught them many useful arts and crafts.

Osiris had a wicked brother, Set, who was jealous of his success. Set murdered his brother the king, cut up his body, and scattered the parts throughout Egypt.

Osiris's faithful wife Isis searched out the scattered remains and, with the help of the jackal-headed god Anubis, was able to put Osiris's body back together and make him live again. However, Osiris could no longer rule over the living. He therefore became god of the dead and judge of souls.

Osiris's son Horus hunted down Set and eventually killed him. In the battle Set put out his nephew's eye. The "eye of Horus" figures prominently in Egyptian art. After avenging his father, Horus became king of Egypt.

The Osiris-Isis-Horus myth was told and retold throughout Ancient Egypt's three-thousand-year history. Long after the fall of Egypt there were temples dedicated to Osiris and Isis all over the Middle East, in Greece, and even in Rome.

Osiris and Isis

23

This Life and the Next

You've heard about mummies and tombs. You hear so much about dead Egyptians, you might get the idea that they were a gloomy people obsessed with death. Not at all. For most of their long history the people of Ancient Egypt were peaceful, prosperous, and cheerful. They enjoyed life in this world and expected to go on enjoying the same sort of life in the next world. They did not fear death.

Egyptians believed that after death a person's spirit, or *ka*, remained near the body. If the body decayed or was destroyed, the spirit would have no place to go. That's why so much time and effort went into preserving a corpse.

The houses Egyptians built were meant to last for only one lifetime. Even the houses of the rich were built from ordinary materials like brick and wood. In hot, dry Egypt people spent most of their time out of doors anyway, so they didn't need large elaborate houses. But the tombs they built were meant to last for eternity.

Kings and nobles were buried with their gold and jewels, their furniture and other household goods. The Egyptians believed that in the next life they would need all of the things they enjoyed in this life.

Rich tombs were stockpiled with enormous quantities of food. Family members and priests brought offerings to the tombs. Sculptures and paintings were also supposed to provide the spirit with what it needed.

Today we say, "You can't take it with you." But the Egyptians believed that you could take it with you—and they tried to.

How They Lived

Hieroglyphic texts tell us that each Egyptian workman was given three loaves of bread, two jugs of beer, and a bunch of onions to eat every day. The bread and beer were made from the grain that grew so abundantly along the Nile. Onions, figs, dates, olives, fish caught in the Nile, and birds trapped in the river's marshes were also a regular part of Egyptians' meals. When an Egyptian gave a party for his friends it was considered polite to eat and drink until you felt sick. But it was not always considered wise. A popular saying was, "Do not drink too much beer, for you will not remember what you have said."

In the hot climate the average Egyptian didn't wear much. What he or she did wear was generally made from linen—the finest cloth in the world. The basic article of clothing for men and women, from farmer to pharaoh, was a short skirt tied in front like a loincloth.

Both men and women wore jewelry, as much as they could afford. But the necklaces and pins were not worn for their beauty alone. They were believed to have magical powers as well.

The Egyptians were among the world's cleanest people. They bathed often, and rubbed their bodies with a huge variety of different oils and perfumes. They sucked on little candies to sweeten their breath. Women colored their lips with red paste and used red paint to dye their fingernails and toenails and stain the palms of their hands and soles of their feet. Both men and women used a lot of eye makeup, which also protected against the eye infections so common in Egypt.

Men and women curled their hair, and when it began to go gray they colored it. Men who feared they were going bald rubbed their scalps with a greasy mixture containing, among other things, hedgehog bones. If all else failed, they wore wigs.

Breakdown and Recovery

"**R**obbers are everywhere . . . the Nile is in flood, yet no one plows . . . every man says: 'We do not know what has happened throughout the land.' "

These gloomy observations are part of a long lament attributed to an Egyptian who lived around 2270 B.C. He lived at a time when the power of the kings, which had reached unprecedented heights under Snefru and Khufu, had begun to break down. Local rulers seized power in their own provinces.

This period of confusion lasted about one hundred years. Then a new series of powerful rulers arose in Thebes, an obscure town in Upper Egypt.

The Theban monarchs began a period of stability and glory for Egypt called The Middle Kingdom. They also began to worship a new god called Amen.

The proud priests of Re, who had been chief god for five hundred years, had to accept this upstart deity favored by the new kings. The two gods were worshiped as one—Amen-Re.

The Middle Kingdom monarchs never had the unquestioned authority of earlier kings. The royal palace was the scene of plots and attempts to overthrow the king. King Amenemhat, who barely survived an assassination attempt, advised his son, "Be on guard against subordinates . . . trust not a brother, know not a friend. . . ." The life of the god-king at that period was not an easy one.

The Foreign Conquerors

Because of its geographic location, Egypt remained secure and stable for many centuries. The country is uniquely isolated. On three sides there are enormous deserts, only sparsely populated by nomads. On the fourth side is the Mediterranean Sea. No ancient nation had a navy large enough to launch an invasion of Egypt. But for a long time people had been filtering down from the area that is now Israel, Syria, and Jordan. They traveled across the Sinai desert and settled in the delta region of Egypt.

When dissension and weakness overwhelmed the Middle Kingdom monarchs, as it did around 1786 B.C., the newcomers seized power. First they took over areas in the delta, then extended their influence throughout Upper Egypt. These usurpers were called the Hyksos, or Rulers of Foreign Lands. Though they tried to adopt Egyptian titles and customs, the Egyptians, who had never been conquered before, hated the foreigners.

The Hyksos had new and superior weapons like the bronze sword and the horse-drawn war chariot. They were able to dominate Egypt for about 150 years, but their rule never really took root. Finally the Egyptians, led once again by the princes of Thebes, drove out the foreigners and chased them all the way back across the Sinai. By 1555 B.C. Egypt was once again ruled by native Egyptians—and now they were armed with new weapons and had developed a taste for foreign conquest.

The Valley of the Kings

The pyramids were marvelous structures. Yet they failed utterly in their main purpose of protecting the bodies of the dead kings. All of the pyramids were robbed, sometimes just a few years after they were built. Still, the Egyptians kept on building pyramids for a thousand years.

Finally King Thutmose I broke with tradition. He decided to build a secret tomb. The site was a remote and barren valley on the western side of the Nile near Thebes. There was only one narrow passage into the valley. The king's chief architect boasted, "I attended to the excavation of the cliff tomb of His Majesty alone, no one seeing and no one hearing . . ." Of course hundreds of workmen had labored to build the tomb so its location could not have been entirely secret. But a serious effort at hiding the tomb had been made.

After Thutmose I, most of the major kings of Egypt had their tombs cut into the cliffs of that same valley. It came to be known as the Valley of the Kings. But in the end those tombs were no more successful at protecting the mummies than the pyramids had been.

The Tomb Robbers

Tomb robbing was big business in Ancient Egypt, particularly at times when the government was weak and unable to guard the burial sites. Neither fear of the gods nor fear of punishment stopped the gangs of plunderers. Often the robbers were aided by corrupt priests and officials who were supposed to protect the tombs. However, not all those who guarded the mummies were corrupt. Priests in the Valley of the Kings sometimes interrupted the robbers and resealed the tombs. It was a hopeless task, because sooner or later the thieves would come back.

In desperation the priests began moving royal mummies from tombs they believed to be threatened to other hiding places. A record of the places the mummies had been moved to was written on their wrappings. Many of the royal mummies, including those of some of Egypt's greatest kings, were crammed into a small underground chamber that could be reached only by a narrow 30-foot shaft.

There the mummies lay undisturbed for nearly three thousand years until they were discovered, in 1871, by a group of modern tomb robbers. These robbers were slowly selling off the contents of their find when Egyptian authorities arrested them and forced them to reveal their secret.

A young man named Emil Brugsch, who worked for the Cairo Museum, was sent to investigate. Brugsch was lowered into the hole and came upon a narrow chamber: ". . . every inch . . . was covered with coffins and antiquities of all kinds. My astonishment was so overpowering I scarcely knew whether I was awake or whether it was only a dream. . . . All the mummies well preserved, thirty-six coffins all belonging to kings, or queens or princes or princesses."

Queen Hatshepsut before her temple

The Queen Who Became King

From the earliest time it had been the tradition that only a man could rule Egypt. But relationships in the Egyptian royal family could become complicated, and this tradition was shattered when a very successful female ruler came to power.

Around 1495 B.C. King Thutmose I died. He left behind a daughter, Hatshepsut, and a son named after his father. To strengthen the boy's claim to the throne he was married to his half-sister, Hatshepsut. He ruled under the name Thutmose II. But Thutmose II was weak, and completely over-shadowed by the strong-willed Hatshepsut. He reigned only a few years and at his death he left a young son who was the offspring of a harem girl. Though this son inherited the royal title of Thutmose III, the real ruler was Hatshepsut. She had herself formally proclaimed "king." From that

time on, the royal sculptors often showed her with a beard.

Although scribes described her as a "raging crocodile," a compliment meaning that she was fierce and warlike, her reign was a relatively secure one. She sent trading expeditions all along the coast of Africa, extending Egypt's commercial contacts farther than ever before. She also built an immense temple at Thebes that is still considered one of the great glories of Egyptian architecture.

Historian James Henry Breasted called her "The first great woman in history."

After twenty-two years of ruling Egypt this remarkable woman disappears from the records. It is unknown whether she died of natural causes or was killed or otherwise thrust aside. Waiting in the background was Thutmose III, no longer a boy, but a man of nearly thirty.

The Warrior King

Thutmose III had not wasted the years he spent in Hatshepsut's shadow. He had been a general in the army. When he became sole ruler of Egypt, he quickly became its greatest warrior king. What Thutmose III really thought of Hatshepsut we will never know, but by the end of his reign his workmen had chiseled her name out of inscriptions and smashed statues of her. Hatshepsut's name was removed from official records of the royal family.

The king used most of his formidable energy attacking Egypt's neighbors. Bold, almost reckless in battle, Thutmose had complete faith in the efficiency of his army and its most powerful weapon—the horse-drawn war chariot.

The chariot that had first been used by the Hyksos to defeat the Egyptians had been made lighter and more maneuverable. It was essentially a fast-moving platform on wheels from which a skilled archer could loose a murderous rain of arrows on the enemy. Following the chariots were more archers. Mopping up was done by foot soldiers armed with swords and spears and clad in leather or wadded cloth thick enough to stop enemy arrows.

Year after year Thutmose led his armies northward into Syria and beyond. He gave the unruly chiefs and princes a beating they did not forget for centuries. By the end of his long life Thutmose III had established Egypt as a true empire—probably the most powerful, and certainly the richest, nation in the ancient world.

Thutmose III leading his army into battle

The Spirit of Aten

For centuries the Egyptians had worshiped their many gods. The priesthoods, particularly the priesthood of Amen-Re, had grown rich and powerful. Then one king tried to change everything.

Amenhotep IV came to the throne at a time when the power of the Egyptian Empire was at its height. His name meant "Amen is Satisfied." After a few years he began to worship only one god —the Aten. He even changed his name to Akhenaten, which means "Spirit of Aten." The Aten was represented as the sun with rays ending in small hands extending from it. Some of the hands held the *ankh,* a symbol of life. No one knows why Akhenaten adopted this new religion or where it came from. But he was completely devoted to it.

Akhenaten moved his capital from Thebes, the city of Amen, to a newly built city of Aten, which he vowed never to leave. He said his religion

"lived on truth." His artists were inspired by the idea of truth. Instead of showing the king in the stiff, formal style that had endured for centuries, he was shown in informal poses, eating or playing with his children. And the artists did not flatter the king. He appears as a long-faced, potbellied, almost grotesque man. Very few kings in history have allowed their artists that sort of freedom. However, Akhenaten's beautiful queen, Nefertiti, was the subject of the most famous and loveliest portrait bust ever fashioned.

The pharaoh wrote several hymns to Aten in which the sun is seen as the gentle source of all created things.

But Akhenaten was more of a poet and a dreamer than a ruler. On the borders there was revolt against Egyptian authority. Lost in worship, the king paid no attention to repeated pleas for help.

In Egypt itself the Aten religion never took hold beyond the royal family and loyal members of the court. The resentful Amen priesthood and the Egyptian people, who wanted their old gods back, ultimately doomed the religious revolution.

The Forgotten King

Before his death Akhenaten tried to compromise with the priests of Amen. Nefertiti, however, remained strong in the new faith. She moved to her own palace, where she continued pure Aten worship.

Akhenaten died around 1359 B.C. We do not know how he died. His tomb was never used. His mummy has never been found. The throne eventually passed to a boy of about nine, probably a younger brother of the dead king. His name was Tutankh*aten*. Considering the religious turmoil and hostility to Aten worship, the boy's advisers decided his name should be changed to Tutankh*amen*. This was a signal that the priests of Amen were again in control.

Tutankhamen lived for only eight more years. His body indicates that he died of a head wound caused by the thrust of a spear or arrow. Perhaps he was wounded in battle or while hunting, or perhaps he was assassinated. He was buried quickly in a modest tomb. Tutankhamen was the last king directly related to Akhenaten. After his death a new line of kings, dedicated to the old gods, took over. They tried to destroy all references to Akhenaten and Tutankhamen.

Akhenaten was too important to be forgotten. When it was necessary to refer to him in the records he was called simply "the Criminal." Tutankhamen, who had accomplished little, was practically ignored. It was his very obscurity that made robbers overlook his tomb, and allowed it to be

Howard Carter and Lord Carnarvon excavating the tomb of King Tutankhamen

the only unplundered royal tomb to be discovered in modern times. By a twist of fate this forgotten king of Ancient Egypt is now better known than any other.

King Tut's Curse

The tomb of King Tutankhamen was opened on November 26, 1922, by Howard Carter who discovered it. Standing at Carter's side was Lord Carnarvon, the wealthy Englishman who had put up the money for Carter's work. Less than four months later Carnarvon lay dying in an Egyptian hospital. He was only fifty-seven years old, and his death was sudden and unexpected, the result of an infection from an insect bite.

Rumors began to fly that he had fallen victim to an ancient curse. It was said that carved above the door of the tomb were these words: DEATH SHALL COME ON SWIFT WINGS TO HIM WHO DISTURBS THE PEACE OF THE KING.

The story of "King Tut's curse" and all the people killed by it has been handed down ever since. But there never was any curse. No such carving was ever found. Egyptians did not put curses on their tombs. Carnarvon died unexpectedly, but Carter lived for another seventeen years. Carnarvon's two children, who were at the tomb when it was opened, lived to be nearly ninety.

Still, the tale of the "curse" is told over and over again. Howard Carter got so tired of being asked about "the curse" that whenever someone brought it up, he would just turn around and walk away.

"Everywhere the Glint of Gold..."

That's what Howard Carter said when he first looked into King Tutankhamen's tomb. No one has ever used gold more lavishly or expertly than the Egyptians. Gold was found in the sand along the Nile in Nubia, the land just south of Egypt. *Nub* is the Egyptian word for gold. Gold was also dug from the earth in northern Egypt near the Red Sea.

The yellow metal that seemed to shine like the sun was identified with the sun god and with the pharaoh. The king appeared before his people surrounded by golden splendor. He sat on a throne sheathed with gold; he wore a golden headdress and a golden collar. His sandals were golden. Even the false beard he often wore was made of gold.

Though King Tutankhamen's tomb was modest, the coffin itself was of solid gold that weighed nearly twenty-five hundred pounds. When the coffin was opened it revealed a gold death mask, a striking portrait of the young king. The mask is one of the greatest golden treasures ever.

The Egyptians also used gold to bribe neighboring kingdoms to keep them friendly. The ruler of one small kingdom complained in a letter to Akhenaten that he wasn't getting enough gold. In his father's day, the ruler said, the pharaoh sent lots of gold. Now he sends only a little. The ruler ends his letter with the demand: "Send me much gold."

Akhenaten's reply, if any, has never been found.

The First Peace Treaty

Statue of Rameses II

"**O**ne gets so tired of Rameses," one traveler in Egypt complained. "His face, his figure, and/or his name are plastered over half the wall surfaces still standing in Egypt; at least it seems that way."

Rameses II died in 1213 B.C. He was eighty-six years old and had ruled for sixty-seven of them. He was the last truly great ruler of Egypt. During his long reign he was a monumental builder. Temples and statues to his greater glory are scattered up and down the Nile. Rameses did not hesitate to tear down monuments built by earlier kings and use the stone for his own monuments. When he didn't actually tear a monument down he had his own name chiseled in the place of others.

Rameses loved to be hailed as a great conqueror. A long epic poem describing his victory over the Hittite Empire (part of modern Turkey) at the battle of Kadesh (Lebanon) is inscribed on the walls of at least three different temples. In truth the battle was nearly a disaster for the Egyptians and Rameses was lucky to escape alive.

Rameses signed a peace treaty with the Hittites. Copies of the treaty in both Egyptian and Hittite have been found. The treaty was carefully observed by both nations for over seventy years, giving the Middle East one of the longest periods of tranquillity in its generally turbulent history. Rameses even married a Hittite princess, and claimed to love her better than all his other wives, who were Egyptians.

Alexander the Great

After the time of Rameses II, Egypt went into a long, slow decline. It was conquered by Libyans, Nubians, and Persians. In the year 332 B.C. the army of Alexander the Great entered Egypt. He had a great respect for the ancient civilization, and was hailed more as a liberator than a conqueror.

Alexander laid plans for a city in the delta to be called Alexandria. He had chosen the site for his city well, for it was to become a world center of commerce and culture.

While in Egypt there occurred one of the most curious episodes in Alexander's career. He made a dangerous 500-mile trek through the desert with just a few companions to visit a remote shrine of the god Amen. At the shrine the god was supposed to answer questions about the future. Alexander never revealed the question he asked or the answer he got. But most people believe the oracle told him that he was a god and destined to conquer the world. After the visit Alexander demanded that his troops treat him like a god.

In his short life Alexander actually did conquer much of the known world. He died when he was only thirty-three. His generals divided up his vast empire. One of the generals, Ptolemy, claimed the richest part of the empire, Egypt. He also took the conqueror's body and installed it in a magnificent tomb in Alexandria.

Alexander the Great before the shrine of Amen

Cleopatra and the Romans

The Ptolemy family was not Egyptian. Like Alexander himself they originally came from Macedon, a region just north of Greece. They spoke and wrote the Greek language. But when they took over Egypt they adopted all the trappings of the Egyptian pharaohs of old. They wore Egyptian clothes, worshiped Egyptian gods, and demanded that the people of Egypt treat them as gods.

Egypt under the Ptolemies was rich, but not powerful. The banks of the Nile still produced more grain than any other place on earth. Merchants and scholars flocked to Alexandria. The library at Alexandria was the greatest storehouse of knowledge in the ancient world. But Egypt didn't have an army or a navy. It certainly could not stand for long against the expanding military power of the Roman Empire.

After the death of Ptolemy XII, the throne passed to the boy Ptolemy XIII and his very clever and ambitious older sister, Cleopatra. Cleopatra knew that if Egypt was to survive as an independent kingdom it would need powerful friends in Rome. She captivated the Roman conqueror Julius Caesar when he visited Egypt, and she went with him to Rome. She even bore him a son.

But Caesar was assassinated and Rome was torn by civil war. Cleopatra then allied herself with Caesar's friend Mark Antony, who was contending for supreme power in Rome. Their relationship was partly practical and political—she needed Roman protection; he needed Egyptian wealth.

Queen Cleopatra

But the Egyptian queen and the Roman warrior also developed a deep love for each other. They had several children.

The Roman civil war dragged on for years. In the end Antony and Cleopatra lost. It was a Roman custom for losing generals to commit suicide by stabbing themselves. That is what Antony did. Cleopatra knew that her fate would be grim if she was captured by her Roman enemies, so she too committed suicide. According to legend she allowed herself to be bitten by a poisonous snake, a symbol of Egypt.

The Romans decided that an independent Egypt would always be a potential threat to their power. In 30 B.C. Egypt was made a province of the Roman Empire. It was no longer ruled by a god-king but by a governor sent from Rome. Thus the kingdom of Egypt, which had endured for over three thousand years, finally came to an end.

But our fascination with Ancient Egypt never ends. Each year tourists still flock to the land of the Nile to marvel at the pyramids and other monuments. Museums all over the world display Egyptian art and Egyptian mummies. And while archaeologists have been digging in the sands of Egypt for centuries now, new discoveries are still being made. The story of Ancient Egypt is not yet complete.

Index

About the Author

Daniel Cohen is a well-known author of over one hundred books—many of them on science, history, and the mysteries of the unknown. Several of his works have been cited as outstanding books for children by various organizations including the Children's Book Council, the National Science Teachers' Association, and the New York Public Library. He is also the author of *Dinosaurs* and *Prehistoric Animals* for Doubleday.

Mr. Cohen resides in Port Jervis, New York, with his wife.

About the Artist

Gary A. Lippincott is an award-winning illustrator who graduated from the Maryland Institute College of Art in Baltimore with a bachelor of fine arts in painting. Gary's love for painting historical scenes comes through in the illustrations for this book, his fourth for children. He is a member of the Western Massachusetts Illustrators' Guild, and when not working on his paintings, he finds time to devote to magic and scuba diving, two of his favorite pastimes.

The artist currently resides in Spencer, Massachusetts.

MAJOR EVENTS IN THE HISTORY OF ANCIENT EGYPT

OLD KINGDOM

UNIFICATION UNDER KING NARMER — 3,100 B.C.

2,700 B.C. — STEPPED PYRAMID OF ZOSER IS BUILT

PYRAMIDS OF GIZA CONSTRUCTED — 2,500 B.C.

FIRST INTERMEDIATE PERIOD 2,200–2,050 B.C.

POLITICAL TURMOIL, TEMPLES RANSACKED, TOMBS AND STATUES DESTROYED

PERIOD OF CULTURAL SPLENDOR

MIDDLE KINGDOM 2,050–2,000 B.C.

SECOND INTERMEDIATE PERIOD 1,800–1,580 B.C.

INVASION OF HYKSOS

NEW KINGDOM

HYKSOS DRIVEN OUT OF EGYPT

1,580 B.C.

1,501–1,447 B.C. — REIGN OF HATSHEPSUT AND THUTMOSE III